Blink of an Eye
SUPERFAST Animals!

Peregrine Falcon
Dive, Dive, Dive!

by Natalie Lunis

Consultant: J. Peter Jenny
President & CEO of The Peregrine Fund
www.peregrinefund.org

BEARPORT
PUBLISHING

NEW YORK, NEW YORK

Credits

Cover, © M. Delpho/Arco Images/Alamy; TOC, ©mlorenz/Shutterstock; 4–5, © M. Delpho/Arco Images/Alamy; 6, © Mark Salter/Alamy; 7, © Dietmar Nill/ Foto Natura/Minden Pictures; 8T, © Tracy Ferrero/Alamy; 8B, © Konrad Wothe/Minden Pictures; 9, © Martin Dohrn/Nature Picture Library; 10, © M. Delpho/Blickwinkel/age fotostock; 11, © N. N. Birks/Ardea; 12T, © X. Eichaker/Peter Arnold Inc.; 12B, © Malcolm McHugh/Alamy; 13, © Dietmar Nill/Nature Picture Library; 14T, © Holly Kuchera/Shutterstock; 14B, © Dan Sullivan/Alamy; 15, © age fotostock/SuperStock; 16T, © Associated Press/AP Images; 16B, © Steve Hopkin/Ardea; 17, © John Hawkins/FLPA/Minden Pictures; 18, © Jim West/Alamy; 19, © Dave Watts/Nature Picture Library; 20, © Sandor H. Szabo/epa/Corbis; 21, © U.S. Air Force photo by Airman 1st Class Grovert Fuentes-Contreras; 22, © M. Delpho/Arco Images/Alamy; 23TL, © Holly Kuchera/Shutterstock; 23TC, © Dietmar Nill/Nature Picture Library; 23TR, © Elnur/Shutterstock; 23BL, © Dietmar Nill/ Foto Natura/Minden Pictures; 23BR, © Malcolm McHugh/Alamy.

Publisher: Kenn Goin
Editorial Director: Adam Siegel
Creative Director: Spencer Brinker
Design: Debrah Kaiser
Photo Researcher: James O'Connor

Library of Congress Cataloging-in-Publication Data

Lunis, Natalie.
  Peregrine falcon : dive, dive, dive! / by Natalie Lunis.
    p. cm. — (Blink of an eye: superfast animals)
  Includes bibliographical references and index.
  ISBN-13: 978-1-936087-93-8 (library binding)
  ISBN-10: 1-936087-93-6 (library binding)
  1. Peregrine falcon—Juvenile literature. I. Title.
  QL696.F34L865 2011
  598.9'6—dc22
                          2010008023

For more information, write to Bearport Publishing Company, Inc., 101 Fifth Avenue, Suite 6R, New York, New York 10003. Printed in the United States of America in North Mankato, Minnesota.

062010
042110CGA

10 9 8 7 6 5 4 3 2 1

Contents

A Fast Falcon

The peregrine (PEH-ruh-grin) falcon is the fastest animal in the world.

It can fly at a speed of 68 miles per hour (109 kph).

Many birds can fly that fast.

However, the falcon can also dive through the air at an even more amazing speed—200 miles per hour (322 kph).

No other animal can do that!

A baseball pitcher's fastball flies at a top speed of about 104 miles per hour (167 kph). The world's fastest roller coaster travels at a top speed of 128 miles per hour (206 kph). A diving peregrine falcon is faster than both.

Baseball Pitcher
104 mph/167 kph

Roller Coaster
128 mph/206 kph

Diving Peregrine Falcon
200 mph/322 kph

Homes in High Places

Peregrine falcons can be found in many parts of the world.

They usually live in places with steep, rocky cliffs.

There, high above the ground, they make their nests on **ledges**.

From these nesting places, they have a good view of the land spread out below.

Peregrine Falcons in the Wild

■ **Where peregrine falcons live**

Peregrine falcons do not build a nest out of dried grass or twigs, as many other birds do. Instead, they make a nest by scraping out a shallow hole in the dirt, sand, or gravel found on their rocky ledges.

City Life

Some peregrine falcons settle down in big cities.

They find places to nest on the ledges of tall buildings.

Because there are so many pigeons, starlings, and other birds flying below, the falcons find plenty to eat, too.

starling

pigeon

8

New York, Los Angeles, Baltimore, Cleveland, and Toronto are just a few of the many cities where peregrine falcons live and nest.

9

A High-Speed Hunt

A peregrine falcon is a **bird of prey**.

It hunts and kills other birds for food—almost always in midair.

The fast-flying falcon has excellent eyesight.

As soon as it spots a bird flying by, it takes off, and the high-speed chase begins.

A peregrine falcon can see five times farther than a person.

Daring Dives

If a bird is flying in front of a peregrine falcon during a hunt, the falcon speeds up and grabs it with its **talons**.

If the bird is flying below, the falcon folds its wings in, taking the shape of a speeding bullet.

It dives headfirst toward its victim.

Sometimes the falcon grabs the bird in its talons.

Other times, it knocks the victim to the ground with its closed talons.

Then it swoops down to get its meal.

diving falcon

talons

A peregrine falcon takes a bird it has caught to a high spot on a cliff or to a tree branch. Then the falcon eats it. If the bird is too heavy to carry, the peregrine eats it on the ground.

13

Dangerous Enemies

Speed and sharp talons are not a peregrine falcon's only weapons.

The birds also have very sharp **beaks**.

The only enemies that are tough enough to hunt them are larger birds of prey, such as the great horned owl and the golden eagle.

Yet peregrines almost disappeared during the 1960s and 1970s.

The danger that nearly wiped them out came from a different kind of enemy—a poison called DDT.

beak

great horned owl

golden eagle

Great horned owls and golden eagles usually hunt young, not yet fully grown falcons. Sometimes, however, a great horned owl will try to grab and kill an adult peregrine falcon at night, while the falcon is sleeping.

15

The Danger of DDT

airplane spraying DDT

Starting in the 1940s, DDT was sprayed on farm **crops** to kill insects.

Many kinds of birds ate insects that had DDT in them, and peregrine falcons ate many of these birds.

The DDT that got into the falcons' bodies did not kill them, but it did harm the eggs they laid.

The shells were so thin that they cracked when the falcon parents sat on them.

The baby falcons inside the broken eggs never hatched.

DDT caused these eggs to crack.

Peregrine falcons lay three or four eggs at a time. The mother and father take turns sitting on the eggs to keep them warm.

eggs

Making a Comeback

After the use of DDT began, people noticed that there were fewer and fewer peregrine falcons around.

Luckily, scientists worked hard to save the birds.

They rescued falcons and cared for the eggs they laid.

When enough young falcons had hatched, the scientists let them go free.

Before long, the birds they had returned to the wild started families of their own.

By the 1980s, peregrines were seen soaring over open country and city streets once again.

baby peregrine falcon being cared for by a scientist

In 1972, the United States government no longer allowed DDT to be used. This change helped the peregrine falcon make a strong comeback.

peregrine falcon feeding young

High-Speed Helpers

People have admired peregrine falcons for a long time.

Starting more than 3,000 years ago, humans trained them to help hunt birds in a sport called falconry.

Today, falcons are being trained to help in a new way.

At some airports, they hunt birds that might get in the way of planes that are taking off or landing.

By doing so, falcons give people one more reason to admire their awesome speed and daring dives.

peregrine falcon
working at an airport

Peregrine falcons are popular with city bird-watchers. Some of them have even set up "nestcams"—webcams that allow people to watch the peregrines and their nests on a computer at any time of day.

Built for Speed

What makes a peregrine falcon fly and dive so fast? Here is how different parts of the bird's body help it reach its amazing speeds.

curved, pointed wings with very stiff feathers provide power when flapping during flight; they also help with high-speed turns

large heart and lungs send muscles the large amounts of oxygen they need to move and hold in the wings

strong muscles in the chest help flap wings during flight; they also help hold in wings during a dive

tail feathers fold in during a fast dive and can also fan out for braking when slowing down

Glossary

beaks (BEEKS) the hard, sharp parts of birds' mouths, often pointy or shaped like a hook

bird of prey (BIRD UHV PRAY) a bird that hunts birds and sometimes other animals for food

crops (KROPS) plants that are grown and gathered, often for food

ledges (LEJ-iz) narrow shelf-like parts that stick out from the side of a cliff or a building

talons (TAL-uhnz) sharp, curved claws on the feet of some kinds of birds

23

Index

Read More

Jenkins, Priscilla Belz. *Falcons Nest on Skyscrapers*. New York: HarperCollins (1996).

Kops, Deborah. *Falcons*. Woodbridge, CT: Blackbirch (2000).

Wechsler, Doug. *Peregrine Falcons*. New York: PowerKids Press (2001).

Learn More Online

To learn more about peregrine falcons, visit
www.bearportpublishing.com/BlinkofanEye

About the Author

Natalie Lunis has written many science and nature books for children. She lives in the Hudson River Valley, just north of New York City.